*Youthful Verses*

# Marina Tsvetaeva

# *Youthful Verses*

*translated from the Russian by*
Christopher Whyte

Shearsman Books

First published in the United Kingdom in 2020 by
Shearsman Books Ltd
PO Box 4239
Swindon
SN3 9FN

Shearsman Books Ltd Registered Office
30–31 St. James Place, Mangotsfield, Bristol BS16 9JB
*(this address not for correspondence)*

www.shearsman.com

ISBN 978-1-84861-731-5

# Contents

# Introduction

The poems in this collection show a youthful Marina Tsvetaeva against a background of normality – if anything about this poet can be described as normal! – which must inevitably appear fragile and provisional in retrospect. The twin revolutions of 1917, war communism and near impossible living conditions in Moscow of the "plague year" 1919, then emigration, isolation and wracking poverty in the Paris years after 1925 cast an inevitable shadow back from the future.

Tsvetaeva's father Ivan Tsvetaev (1847–1913), the son of a country priest, began his university career in Latin literature before moving to the study of antiquities, and was the founder of what became the capital city's Pushkin Museum. From 1889 he occupied the chair of Art History and Theory at Moscow University. Her mother Maria Meyn (1868–1906), hopelessly in love with a married man and a gifted pianist, knowingly contracted in 1891 a marriage of duty to a widower with 2 children who was still very much in love with his first wife. Tsvetaeva described her in a letter to Vassily Rozanov dated April 8th 1914:

> Mama was an only child. Her mother, from a princely Polish family, died age twenty-six. Grandfather dedicated his whole life to Mama, who at her mother's death was a very small child. Her life was divided between grandfather and a Swiss governess – isolated, fantastical, frequently ill, not childlike, a life of books. Age seven she knew all of world history and mythology, dreamt of heroes, played the piano splendidly. [...]
>
> The whole spirit of her upbringing was Germanic. Drunk on music, a *colossal talent* (I shall never again hear anyone play the piano and the guitar as she did!), gifted in languages, an amazing memory, a magnificent command of words, poems in Russian and in German, she also painted. [...]

Her tormented soul lives on in us – but we reveal what she concealed. Her mutiny, her folly, her thirst in us reach the level of a shout.

Maria Meyn died of tuberculosis in 1906, when her daughter was still thirteen. The poet and her sister Anastasia (Asya), two years younger, a writer and a poet herself, subsequently enjoyed a degree of freedom which can be hard to credit across the distance of more than a century, and which became greater still after their father's death in 1913. In summer 1909 Tsvetaeva travelled to Paris, rented rooms in the Rue Bonaparte, and was heartbroken when the woman teaching her French failed to reciprocate a passionate attachment (to Lyudmila Chirikova, November 3rd 1922):

> I lived in Paris – long ago, when I was sixteen, lived alone, no luxuries – it was more a dream of Paris, than Paris itself. (Like my whole life – a dream of life, not life itself!)
>
> Go for my sake to Rue Bonaparte, that's where I lived: 59bis. I chose my lodgings for the name of the street, for then (by the way, that will never change!) more than anyone and anything I loved Napoleon.
>
> Rue Bonaparte – delightfully Catholic and monarchist (légitimiste!), in every building there was an antiques shop.
>
> It would be great if you could go to live there: on the map, it's between two squares, St Germain des Prés and St Germain l'Auxerrois, right on the Seine. – The Quartier Latin.
>
> And, what should attract you more than anything – in each small window, an old man aged one hundred and ten and an old woman aged ninety-nine.

An uncollected poem recalls the Moscow house on Three Ponds Lane, given to Ivan Tsvetaev by the father of his first wife, the opera singer Varvara Dimitriyevna Ilovaysky (1858–1890), to which Marina and Asya returned in autumn 1906 after their mother's death:

You who have not stopped dreaming yet,
whose every movement is subdued,
turn off into Three Ponds Lane
if you love my poetry.

So sunny and so filled with stars
the opening chapters of life's book,
I beg you, before it's too late –
come, take a look at where we lived!

That whole world's going to be destroyed
(nobody must know you're there)
as yet they haven't felled the poplar,
the house which was ours is unsold.

That poplar tree offered its shade
to all our childhood evenings,
glimmering ashen-coloured, silver,
an acacia on either side!

If you hurry, you'll find it there,
that world of irretrievable
miracles in Three Ponds Lane –
turn off into my inmost soul.

*1913?*

An inheritance allowed Marina and Sergey to buy their own home in 1912. Their first daughter Ariadne (Alya) was born on September 5th. In 1914 the young family moved to the house on Borisoglebsky pereulok where Tsvetaeva would remain, living for a period in squalid conditions of near-absolute destitution in the attic, until her emigration from Russia in spring 1922.

When in October 1910 Tsvetaeva published privately her very first book of poems, its reviewers included Maximilian Voloshin (1877–1932), in Simon Karlinsky's words 'a burly, blond-bearded giant', a 'man of uncertain or underdeveloped sexuality, both of whose marriages were of the *mariage blanc* variety', who 'cultivated the friendship of women and poets'. It was at the boarding house in Crimea run by Voloshin and his mother, frequented by a motley, Bohemian crowd of artists and writers, that Tsvetaeva met the man who was to become her husband, Sergey Efron (1893–1941). She recalled the day a decade later, in 1921, at which point they had already been separated for more than three years. She was trapped in Moscow with their two daughters, while he served as an officer in the White Army opposing the Bolsheviks:

Well it was May 5th 1911 – a sunny day – that I saw you for the first time on a bench by the sea. You were sitting next to Lilya, wearing a white shirt. Catching sight of you, I was stunned: 'Can anyone be so beautiful? When you see someone like that it makes you ashamed to walk the earth!'

Tsvetaeva did not tire of retelling the story of how, on meeting Sergey, she asked him to bring her a pebble from the beach. The one he selected convinced her as to the rightness of her choice. To Rozanov she wrote (March 7th 1914):

I am married and have a daughter of a year and a half – Ariadna (Alya), my husband is twenty. He is unusually and nobly handsome, beautiful outside and inside. On his father's side his great-grandfather was a rabbi, on his mother's – a splendid officer in the guard of Nicholas I. In Seryozha are united – brilliantly united – two bloods: Jewish and Russian. He is brilliantly gifted, intelligent, high-minded. And his mother was a beauty and a heroine. […]

He is seriously ill, age sixteen he developed tuberculosis. Now the disease is stationary, but his general state of health is considerably below the average. If only you knew what a fiery, magnanimous, profound youth he is! I tremble for him constantly. The least excitement makes him feverish, he is consumed by a thirst for everything. When we met he was seventeen, I eighteen. In three – nearly three – years of life together, not a single shadow. Our marriage bears so little resemblance to an ordinary marriage, that I don't feel married at all and haven't changed one bit – I love the same things and live in the same way as at seventeen.

We shall never separate. Our meeting was a miracle. I am writing this to you so you don't think of him as a stranger. He is my closest kin for the whole of life. I could never have loved anybody else, in me there is too much melancholy and rebellion. Only next to him can I live as I do – in total freedom.

None – almost none! – of my friends is able to understand my choice. Choice? Good God, as if I had a choice!

Efron's mother had gone into political exile due to her participation in a terrorist group called People's Freedom. She committed suicide in 1910 on finding that her son Constantine had hanged himself in the bathroom of their Paris apartment. Tsvetaeva's bond with Sergey was to persist, through ups and downs, for more than a quarter of a century, until and after his arrest by the KGB in October 1939.

Neither of them viewed it as precluding other, extra-marital attachments. If Efron appears never to have felt an obligation to provide his family with material support, their relationship permitted his wife to engage in a long series of infatuations, of love affairs with and without an element of physical realisation, which nourished her writing and her poetry, and whose cessation she would lament despairingly in her letters to Pasternak of the mid 1920s. Tsvetaeva would later say that early motherhood had ruined her life, always having to lead a child by the hand. In reality, the provision of nannies in a privileged family in pre-Revolutionary Russia meant she retained extended space for her writing, her infatuations, and for interaction with an extensive social and intellectual circle.

Tsvetaeva's mother made sure that her daughters grew up fluent in both German and French. She would appear to have treated Tsvetaeva, who was planned to be a son named Alexander, with exceptional harshness, of which the poet bore the scars throughout her adult life. It issued in an attitude to the self which can best be described as adversarial, oppositional, expressed in an unmistakable tendency to verbal masochism, to self-denunciation through the medium of poetry.

*

Critical orthodoxy dictates that, like the poet, we should prefer the tormented, complex poems from her last two years in Russia and the time of her emigration in Berlin and Prague to the lyrics which make up *Youthful Verses*. She wrote to Lyudmila Chirikova in the letter already quoted:

> You have been of great help to me, now I shall have in my hands my earlier poems, which everybody likes.
> With the new ones (the utterances of a Sibyl) I would fail: no one needs them, since they are written from the other shore: *from Heaven!*

And yet the earlier poems contain many of her most carefully sculpted, eloquent and memorable items. A young woman depicts herself and the people and places she moves among with a degree of vividness and frankness still capable of taking the breath away. Dust has not settled on them.

When she writes from the Paris suburb of Meudon to her Czech friend Anna Teškova in Prague on November 18th 1928, Tsvetaeva's need for this same, unpublished collection has grown still more urgent:

The next request is very important. We are *truly* in dire straits, everything goes on rent and food (horse meat, we can't afford any other), I only get published in *Poslednie Novosti* (the newspaper), but they only accept old poems, from ten years back. [...] Whatever happens, someone must wrest from Mark Lvovich Slonim the manuscript of my *Youthful Verses*. Me writing to him is pointless, as he either doesn't answer, or does nothing. [...] If possible, do this as soon as you can. My only earnings are the weekly poems in *Poslednie Novosti*. *All* of *Youthful Verses* is unpublished, for me and for *Poslednie Novosti* (where they *truly* love the old – i.e. the young! me) a whole treasure store. [...]

If you send me this manuscript you will save me, it contains long poems, 40–50 lines i.e. 40–50 francs a week: money!

The collection as a whole did not achieve publication until 1976, and even then in a version slightly different from the author's final intentions, which correspond to a copy of which Victoria Schweitzer gives a detailed account. This is a typescript, astonishingly in the new spelling which Tsvetaeva never adopted, and which was introduced from February 1918. The lettering is so faint that she had to retrace words, phrases and whole verses in red ink filched from the nationalities bureau where she worked during the winter of 1918–19. Together with the first book of *Milestones*, it was offered to Valery Bryusov for publication in 1919, and rejected.

All the items in *Youthful Verses* are translated here, with the exception of the long poem placed close to midpoint, 'The Enchanter', nowadays classified among Tsvetaeva's verse narratives.

In this, her third collection, Tsvetaeva does not seem to realise that limits have been stipulated as to what a young woman like herself may register and express in her writing. For all her undoubted genius, in her love lyrics before the October Revolution

Anna Akhmatova respected these, remaining more or less within the bounds of what could conventionally be regarded as "women's poetry". Tsvetaeva's gender identification throughout her life was fragile and unstable. She wrote in her notebooks that

> Men and women are not equally akin to me, but equally alien. It's as easy for me to say "you women" as "you men".
> When I say "we women", there's always an element of exaggeration, I'm entertaining myself, playing.

The lyrics of *Youthful Verses* emerge in a utopia where anything can be felt, anything can be said. Only gradually would the twin traumas of revolution and emigration, together with the harsh realities of magazine publication in the emigré press, bring home to Tsvetaeva that this had never been the case. Such freedom of speech constituted a transgression for which a penalty would inevitably be exacted. Reading her across the intervening decades – across the for her proverbial 100 years, after which she would at last encounter the readers and the love and understanding she lacked, and so deserved – we can exult in the directness of utterance she achieved, in the limpid, uncompromising, often confessional declarations which she formulated.

\*

In 1983, having given up hope of publication in Russia for her research into Tsvetaeva's relationship with the seven-years-older, avowedly lesbian poet Sophia Parnok (1885–1933), Sophia Polyakova brought her findings out in the West, with Ann Arbor Press at Michigan University. Polyakova rightly sees the sequence 'With a Woman' (in Russian, literally 'The Girlfriend') as marking a new level of maturity in Tsvetaeva's poetry, which is sustained in the remaining poems of a chronologically ordered collection. The sequence, which Tsvetaeva originally planned to call 'The Mistake' or 'A Mistake' (like the majority of Slavonic languages, Russian possesses neither a definite nor an indefinite article), can be viewed as "queer literature" before the "queer".

It forms part of the flowering of such writing in Russia from the revolution of 1906 until some time after the twin revolutions of 1917. That also included the poetry of Mikhail Kuzmin, who in 1907 published one of Europe's very first explicitly gay novels, *Wings*. If to speak of the book as "gay" is certainly an anachronism, its subtle, unapologetic presentation of male homosexuality in a positive, even proselytising light surely justifies the audacity.

The only occasion on which Tsvetaeva met Kuzmin face to face, during a visit to St Petersburg in the New Year of 1916, shortly preceded the ending of her relationship with Parnok. She describes the circumstances in a letter to Kuzmin. Dated 1921, it survives as a draft in Tsvetaeva's notebooks. The account sets out as a conversation with an imaginary person:

'It was 1916, winter, the first time I visited Petersburg. I was friends then with the Kannegiser family (Good God, Leonid!), they showed me round Petersburg. But I'm shortsighted – it was freezing cold – and Petersburg has so many monuments – and the sleighs went so fast – everything became a blur, all that was left of Petersburg were Pushkin's poems, and Akhmatova's. But no, the fireplaces too – whole oak woods burning! – and white bears on the floor (a white bear in front of a fire! – amazing!) and all the young people had partings in their hair – and volumes of Pushkin in their hands, and varnished nails, and varnished heads – like black mirrors. (Varnish on top, and underneath – a n-tw-t!) How people love poetry there! I've never recited so many poems in my whole life as I did there, in the space of two weeks. And they absolutely don't sleep. The telephone rings at three in the morning. 'Can we come?' 'Of course, of course, everyone's just arriving.' And so on – till the morning. [...]
'It was like this. I'd just arrived. I was with someone, with a woman, actually. Good Lord, how I cried! But that's not important. So, in a word, she was absolutely against me going to that party and kept trying to

persuade me to stay away. She couldn't go herself – she had a headache – and when she had a headache – and she always had – she was unbearable. (A darkened room – blue lamp – me crying…) But I didn't have a headache – I never do! – and I really didn't want to stay at home 1) because of Sonya, then because Kuzmin was going to be there and he'd sing.

'Sonya, I won't go!' 'But why? It makes no difference to me, that's not what I'm like.' 'But I feel sorry for you.' 'There'll be lots of people, you can have fun.' 'No, I feel too sorry for you.' 'I can't stand people feeling sorry for me. Go, just go. Just think, Marina, Kuzmin will be there, he's going to sing.' 'Alright so he's going to sing, and when I come home, you'll be angry with me, and I'll start crying. No way! I'm not going!' 'Marina!'

Leonid's voice: 'Marina Ivanovna! You ready?'

And, without hesitation: 'This very minute!'

[…]

'And your girlfriend?'

'My girlfriend? When I got back, she was already asleep.'

'Where is she now?'

'Somewhere in Crimea. I don't know. In February 1916, that is one month later, we broke up. Basically due to Kuzmin, that is due to Mandelstam, who not having managed to talk things over in Petersburg came to talk them over – in Moscow. When I went away for two days (with Mandelstam), and came back – the first time I left her in years – another woman was sitting on her bed: really tall, stout, dark-haired. – We had been together for a year and a half.

Leonid was the younger son of the Kannegiser family, who hosted the evening. This was where Tsvetaeva first met the poet George Adamovich, also homosexual, with whom she would enter into a bitter polemic in the years of her Paris emigration. According to Simon Karlinsky, Leonid, a budding poet, was very likely having an affair at the time with the peasant poet Sergey Esenin. Adamovich remembered Tsvetaeva and Esenin sitting next to one another. In the wake of the October revolution, Leonid would assassinate the police chief Moisey Uritsky, apparently in revenge for the shooting of his then lover, an army officer named Viktor Pereltsveig, upon which he himself was arrested, tortured and executed.

An idea of the attitude to sexual relations prevalent in Tsvetaeva's ambience can be gleaned from this unattributed testimony in Véronique Lossky's collection of oral reminiscences concerning the poet:

> Marina got to know Sophia Parnok at the Krandiyevskys'. This is the theme of her 'With a Woman' poems. My impression is, it was a purely physical passion.
>
> I think that when Marina married Sergey Efron, it was ordinary love between a man and a woman and, as you know, on such occasions the woman feels nothing.
>
> But with love between women it's different. One woman can let another one feel everything: "jouir"… And Marina's passion for Sophia Parnok was purely physical. But, as happens, since it was only physical, afterwards Marina came to detest Sophia… […]
>
> Generally Marina loved women as she did men. […]
>
> Marina had a generalised attraction to women, from her childhood on. It was not a rebellion against her surroundings, but a personal inclination. […] In general she fell in love often and easily, like me. […]
>
> Now Asya could sleep with everyone, men and women, without loving them. Marina was different, when she didn't love someone, she sought no physical closeness […]
>
> Naturally, she had love stories. And lots of them. Real and unreal. Quite simply, Sergey found that hard. On top of which, he was everywhere 'Marina Tsvetaeva's husband', which is also unpleasant.

When in the course of one of their conversations, Solomon Volkov asks why Tsvetaeva's poetry is 'so rarely erotic', the poet Joseph Brodsky retorts:

My friend, reread Tsvetaeva's poems to Sophia Parnok! When it comes to erotica, she outdoes everyone there – Kuzmin and everyone else included.

The 'With a Woman' cycle benefits from not having a clear narrative sequence, even if it begins with a clamorous description of the thunderbolt first encounter concluding 'because, with a rapture I can't quite believe in,/ you aren't a he!' In modern parlance, the second poem could be said to express Tsvetaeva's understandable confusion about who was "top", who "bottom" in their first night of love: 'What happened? Who came out on top?/ Who was the loser?' The fourth communicates that, no matter how innocent or inexperienced, there is a level at which the younger woman will always prove to be in the right. In the fifth, in a manner reminiscent of the rampant suspicions about Albertine's lesbian promiscuities which bedevil Proust's narrator, the speaker watches her partner pass by in a sleigh with another woman she speaks French to, their laps filled with shopping. Similar perceptions return, in a more resigned fashion, in the penultimate poem. The seventh describes a trip to a monastery far from Moscow in a familiar scenario of 'Things were better when they were worse'. The silence about same sex relationships means 'the fine, strange ladies down from Moscow' enjoy a species of immunity amongst the noisy stallholders 'in russet long coats broad as sails' who swore and 'sold us worthless trinkets'. Retiring for the night to 'the convent's guest quarters', they employ different species of divination, the younger woman having promised to steal an icon of the Virgin Mary the older particularly admired from the church. We read about the 'opal ring' on the 'hand of my whole catastrophe'. The next two items further characterise the speaker's lover, with a forehead like Beethoven's, in her voice 'a gypsy hoarseness'. She is 'a stalk of steel./ Knife-sharp ill-will personified'. The tenth returns to the first meeting, where a bystander provocatively introduced the two, characterised as Orestes and his companion Pylades. The younger lights the older one's cigarette, upon which the latter drops a handkerchief from her bag, like the gauntlet preceding a duel. Already there are signals of repeated break-ups and reconciliations. The last item but one is a listing of other women who have caught the older one's eye, now that things seem definitively over (though the dating shows this was by no means the case – another warning against reading the cycle too slavishly in terms of Tsvetaeva and Parnok's own involvement.)

\*

*Youthful Verses* contains a pair of poems addressed to the poet's daughter Alya (1912–1975). In a letter to the mother of one of the teachers dated November 11th 1923, when Alya's parents briefly placed her as a boarder in the Russian secondary school at Moravská Třebová, Tsvetaeva expressed in distinctly poetic form her sense that her own influence might not always be a desirable one:

> I'm convinced that Alya is doing fine in Třebová, for such a long time she was not a child, she got so little chance simply to have fun during her childhood, while now all at once: friends, days laid out in an organised pattern, games and lessons. If she had carried on living with me, she would have grown up unhappy, I myself was never a proper child, which means I find it hard to understand children: other people's make me afraid, I spoil my own (the one I have). "Physician, heal thyself" (at least where bringing up a child is concerned) can hardly be less appropriate in any case but mine.

Tsvetaeva's letters to Anna Teškova from Paris describe the increasingly painful estrangement which set in between mother and daughter, Alya embracing her father's enthusiasm for the course things were taking in Stalinist Russia, while Tsvetaeva remained stubbornly faithful to her own monarchist, anti-Bolshevik positions. Alya was the first member of the family to return to the Soviet Union in March 1937. Arrested on August 27th 1939, she was forced by torture to sign a false confession and sent to a camp. Her father was arrested on October 10th of the same year. In the latter part of her life, after definitive release and exoneration in 1955, she created an invaluable archive of her mother's writings, finally opened to public scrutiny in the year 2000.

From the time of the first meeting with Sergey till the outbreak of the October revolution, Tsvetaeva spent long periods in the Crimea, in Feodosiya or with the Voloshins in Koktebel', at times together with her husband, at others not. Voloshin's mother resided during the winters in Moscow, where she lived with Sergey's sisters Vera and Lilya. Tsvetaeva's letters to the the sisters offer valuable insights into her life during these years.

Numerous photographs of life in Koktebel' survive. One shows Marina preparing to depart in a carriage drawn by two horses, in front of the rustic stone and mortar exterior of the Voloshin's house with its wooden balcony. Others show large gatherings mainly of younger people, sunburnt and in summer dress, around a table on the terrace or inside, the men reclining languidly, the women bunched together, seemingly more active. Sergey's sisters are present, while Marina stands in perfect profile for the camera. Voloshin's mother Pra is to one side, also in profile. Another shows a bespectacled Marina with a folio volume on her knees in a book-lined study, while Sergey sits opposite on a stool, in a bright smock.

Friends and acquaintances greeted the arrival on the scene of Parnok with consternation. The younger of Sergey's sisters wrote to Voloshin in Paris:

> I have a strange relationship with Marina, but better
> to speak about that later, writing about it is not a good
> idea. I fear that Sergey's whole life will be ruined.

Voloshin's mother wrote at the end of 1914:

> What were the things Seryozha told you? Why are you
> terrified on his behalf? I know he's preparing to enter
> the sanatorium again, but I think he'll change his mind.
> As for Marina, it's appalling: the business is becoming
> absolutely serious. She went off somewhere with Sonya
> for a few days, it was all a huge secret. Sonya has already
> fallen out with her girlfriend, they were living together
> and she has rented her own flat on the Arbat. It really
> troubles and worries me and Lilya, but we are incapable
> of destroying the enchantment.

The same person met Parnok early in February 1915 and came
away with a rather different impression:

> Yesterday I called on Sonya and we talked things
> through for several hours and in what she said there
> were repeated lapses which offended me, and there were
> moments in the conversation when I felt ashamed of
> myself for what I had said about her to other people,
> condemning her, or uttering chill, categorical verdicts
> fit for an executioner.

Polyakova lists a further series of poems as being addressed to
Parnok. They include 'Voices that played at promises', 'In a haze
incense made bluer', where during a church service the speaker's
eyes momentarily catch those of her rival, 'The moon is full, we
wear bear fur', 'Gipsy passion for breaking up!' and the stunning
'The clock has finished chiming':

> The clock has finished chiming – I
> don't know the time.
> In their sockets your eyes are huge,
> rivulets cross the satin of
> your dress. It's hard
> to make you out.

Above the porch next door the light
has been turned off.
Places exist where loving knows
no end. The outline of your face
terrifies me.

Within the twilit room night's in-
divisible.
Transfixed by moonlight, the window's
hollowed-out cavity could be
a block of ice.

"So you give in?" I hear you ask.
"I didn't fight."
Your voice is frozen by the moon,
it could be reaching me across
one hundred miles!

Between us a beam lifts itself,
moves with the world.
Enraged, your hair takes on a glint
of copper, with a darkening tinge –
unbearable.

History's progress is forgotten
in the progress
of a moon the mirror shatters.
Far off a horses' hooves are heard,
a creaking cart.

On the pavement the lamp's gone out.
Progress cut short.
Soon a rooster will proclaim the
time has come for two young women
to separate.

*November 1st 1914*

The temptation to add further items to this list needs careful attention. For example, 'I'm pleased that you are not in love with me' is addressed to M. A. Mintz (1886–1917), who in autumn 1915 became the second husband of Tsvetaeva's sister Asya.

Poised on the brink of apprenticeship and maturity, the cycle 'To P. E.', in a sense prepares the way for 'With a Woman'. Pyotr Yakovlevich Efron (1880–1914) shared his mother's revolutionary politics and fled abroad after the 1907 Moscow uprising. An actor by profession, he returned to Russia in 1913 and died the following year from tuberculosis. A letter Tsvetaeva wrote to him on July 14th 1914 runs as follows:

> Seryozha is twisting and turning on the bed, biting his lips, groaning. I gaze at his long, tender, suffering face and understand everything: my love for him and my love for you.
> Young lads! That is the basis of my love.
> With a pure heart! Savagely misused by life! Boys without a mother! […]
> Were it not for Sergey and Alya, for whom I answer before God, I would joyfully die for you, so you could regain your health. Like that – not hesitating – at the first summons.[…]
> It began with the first minute of enchantment (August or the start of September 1914) and continues with the endlessness of love.

In her notebooks, Tsvetaeva recorded some of Pyotr's words during a visit that same month to the Moscow clinic where he was to die three weeks later:

> When I got those poems, I so wanted to write to you… even just two words, squeezed out of me… two lines, even worthless ones… But no, nothing! And earlier – after your letters! – how often I thought of writing to you… But there would have been so, so very much to

write… And now after the poems only two words would have been needed. But now I cannot even write…

The comradely tone of the earlier items is striking, as is the speaker's aesthetic evaluation of this man, his languid stylishness, his detachment from the world. The fourth is dedicated to his only child Elizaveta, who died in 1909. The fifth addresses all the women who were captivated by his charm, without a hint of rivalry or jealousy on the speaker's part: 'Recall how eagerly you stalked/ each single glance of those two eyes,/ recall the pledges you once made/ in darkest night'. They are imagined kissing the snow above his grave, while beneath the sound of their rustling dresses has him 'trembling head to toe'. Probably the most successful item is the sixth, defying death while at the same time helplessly acknowledging its power, in a tone more appropriate for intimate friends than for lovers.

*

One looks in vain in *Youthful Verses* for poems devoted to a landscape, an anonymous impression, or a passing, momentary thought. These lyrics are inhabited by a sense almost of surprise at the self, coupled with an unwillingness to generalise out of one's own experience. One lyric begins 'What do they see', then does its best to offer an answer, of how the speaker must appear to other eyes. These attempted responses to the question of 'Who am I?' result in extended character sketches which frequently add up to not so subtle self-denigration. Together with surprise, strong reservations are expressed, however humorously and charmingly, about the person Tsvetaeva turns out to be. This 'verbal masochism' characterised Tsvetaeva's poetic voice throughout much of her life – a speaker who, rather than championing herself, prefers to join the opposing side.

The speaker chastises herself for 'Inconsequentiality' or, in 'Prudence – and insane behaviour', speaks of 'the lying instinct Polish great-/ grandmothers bequeathed me'. The enchanting 'Someone among my forebears was a fiddler', with its unexpected, neat readjustment of perspective in the closing line, turns out to be a portait of the speaker and her poetry – anything but a flattering one! A culmination is reached in 'I don't remember who it was', where the speaker confesses that the best thing that could happen would be, being shot to death point-blank. Even the exultant poem of which Nuala Ní Dhomhnaill has produced a fine Irish version, on the basis of the English version by Elaine Feinstein and Angela Livingston, with its clamorous celebration of non-conformist women who reject the roles assigned them, implies that all of this must end very badly indeed. Ultimate retribution will be inescapable:

> Gorgeous sisters, Hell is where
> we shall end up, drinking black pitch,
> who sang the praises of the Lord
> straining our voices till they cracked!
>
> We who would not bend at night
> over spinning-wheels or cradles,
> unsteady boats will transport us
> huddled in our flapping cloaks.
>
> Dressed as soon as we got up
> in thin, delicate Chinese silks,
> around the robbers' bonfire we
> led choruses from paradise.
>
> Hopeless when it came to sewing –
> this way, that way, nothing worked! –
> lording it over the whole world,
> dancing and playing on the flute,
>
> squinting at the constellations
> in rags that barely covered us,
> carousing and promenading
> through the townships of the skies,

strolling beneath a flood of stars
through the orchards of paradise –
darling girls, beloved sisters,
we shall all end up in Hell!

*November 1915*

The self-presentations are accompanied by that constant awareness of the possibility of early death which typifies not a few individuals when they reach the threshold of adulthood. As if, when life displays all its promise and potential, the potential for death were incremented in equal measure: 'Listen to what I'm saying! Love me too/ because I'll die', 'I, who was always rosy-cheeked, will be/ palest of all'. After an opening poem whose original title, subsequently removed, indicated that the subject was the dying hour of the diarist and painter Marie Bashkirtsheff, the second in the whole collection confronts the issue of the speaker's death with an air of doomed rebellion: 'Whatever they let down into/ the earth, it won't be me!' The next speaks from her grave, urging the passer-by not to look too gloomy, but instead to pick one of the particularly juicy strawberries which grow in cemeteries: 'I, too, loved laughing far too much/ when it wasn't allowed!'

In other poems, the speaker's self-characterisation is a passionate self-defence against a male addressee. Here, too, a note of underlying grimness can be detected: 'how menacing and arrow-like// my carefree words were', 'with everything I put on show/ sculpted in desperate stone!' 'Here I lie face down upon/ the bed' is addressed to the law professor Mikhail Solomonovich Feldstein (1884/85–1939), who would marry Sergey's sister Vera, and who, though older and erudite, is encouraged to take the part of a student.

When Tsvetaeva lived in the Crimea, she could hear around her a Turkic language, spoken by the Tartar population. Both the Polish Romantic poet Adam Mickiewicz and Pushkin himself had written of their Crimean sojourns. Tsvetaeva imagines her meeting with the Russian poet against this background. Here, too, we find an extended self-characterisation in terms of the things the speaker loves before, like a pair of children, the poets 'burst out laughing, and then run/ right down the mountain, hand in hand'. Tsvetaeva's nostalgia for the 'Generals of 1812' suggests that her choice of role models respects no boundaries of gender, while the second poet explicitly cited as a model is none other than Lord Byron.

'I'm pleased that you are not in love with me' is a miraculous exercise in sustained, worldly-wise, balanced irony. Given we know the addressee in this case to have been a man, it is worth noting the absolute equality and reciprocity evident in the poem. The 'alas!' close to the end implies that we are in fact dealing with a declaration of love masquerading as a declaration of non-love. 'With incalculable tenderness' captivates with its itemisation of the various objects to be inherited after the speaker's imminent demise, yet ends with a shameless assertion of wilful promiscuity, also an affirmation of her continuing zest for life. Towards the close of the collection, the note of self-denigration fades, even in an apology to the 'sick teenager' whose devotion the speaker, only loving 'words and rings', is incapable of reciprocating.

The almost utopian existence which is the background to these poems contained only as much havoc as the poet was herself able to wreak within it. The very last lines of the book can be read as prophesying the tremendous toll war, revolution and emigration were destined to exact: 'Fate's heavy hand/ caught at my hair as I flew past!'

*Budapest*
*April 2020*

Winged, he approached, and on
the brightness of those eyes the eyelids closed.
Creature composed of flame, you died
at the gloomiest hour.

What compensation can this world
offer in place of two slow, final tears?
He paused to think that over, while
four in the morning chimed.

Without anyone noticing,
he left, taking the most important word
with him, a word nobody heard –
your cry when facing death!

Wrenched, like your soul, from deep within,
your call was lost in a welter of sounds.
Meanwhile you sank, suffused with pink,
into the blur of dawn…

*Moscow 1912*

These lines are dedicated to
whoever's going to make
the coffin where my forehead, high
and hateful, will lie bared.

Changed when there was no need for change,
a ribbon on my brow,
in the coffin my own heart
will not recognise me.

No-one will read what's on my face:
"I've heard, seen everything!
I refuse, even as a corpse,
to be like all the rest!"

Clothed in pure white – a colour I've
detested since childhood! –
lying next to who knows who
till the end of the world.

Look! I didn't agree to this!
It's nothing but a trap!
Whatever they let down into
the earth, it won't be me!

I know! It all burns down to ash!
And my grave won't protect
anything I felt love for
while I was alive.

*Moscow, Spring 1913*

You walk past just the way I would,
with eyes glued to the ground.
That was how I lowered mine!
Passer-by, stop here!

Pick yourself a bunch of butter-
cups and poppies, then
read my name – Marina. See
how old I got to be.

Try to forget this is a grave.
I won't rise, threatening....
I, too, loved laughing far too much
when it wasn't allowed!

The blood would surge into my cheeks
and each single curl bob...
Passer-by, I too was *alive*!
Passer-by, stop here!

Tear yourself a stalk of grass
then pick a strawberry:
only in graveyards do they grow
wild, round and sweet as this.

But don't be gloomy, standing there
with your head downcast.
Think of me light-heartedly,
and then forget the thought.

A ray of sunlight catches you,
you're shrouded in gold motes!...
Just don't be worried by my voice,
emerging from the ground.

*Koktebel' May 3rd 1913*

The poems that I wrote so early on
I didn't even know I was a poet,
a fountain's spray spurting into the air,
sparks a rocket scatters,

little devils bursting through the doors
of sanctuaries filled with sleep and incense,
my poems about being young and dying –
poems nobody reads! –

tossed to one side in dusty warehouses
where no-one came for them, and no-one will,
vintage wines of incalculable worth –
my poems' time will come!

*Koktebel', May 13th 1913*

The veins of an already sunburnt hand
are filled with sunlight, not with blood.
And I'm left face to face with the great love
I bear towards this soul of mine.

I count a hundred, waiting for a cricket,
tear a blade of grass and chew...
– Strange to perceive, so powerfully and simply,
the transience of life – and mine.

*May 15th 1913*

Were you, proceeding beyond me towards
dubious enchantments I know nothing of,
to get even the slightest inkling how
much fire, how much life squandered uselessly,

how much heroic ardour I expend
upon a passing shadow, or a rustle,
the useless detonations which reduced
my heart to ashes, all to no avail!

Train after train speeds onwards through the night,
conveying sleep itself towards a station...
And nonetheless, I'm perfectly aware
that, even if you did, you couldn't tell

why it is the words I utter through
the smoke of cigarettes I can't put down
should be so harsh, how menacing and grim
the melancholy in my fair head is!

*May 17th 1913*

You saw me as a little boy
running past playfully
and would chuckle soberly
at the grim things I said:

"Naughtiness is my life, my name!
If you're not stupid, laugh!"
You didn't see the weariness
behind my whitened lips.

Unable to resist the draw
of two huge, moonlike eyes
you found me too young all the same,
and far too rosy-cheeked!

Melting faster than snow, but with
a core of steel – a ball
taking a running jump, to land
on the piano strings,

sand that grates against the teeth,
steel scratching upon glass…
You alone failed to guess
how menacing and arrow-like

my carefree words were, how my rage
camouflaged tenderness –
with everything I put on show
sculpted in desperate stone!

*May 29th 1913*

Here I lie face down upon
the bed – seething with rage!
Why was it you could not agree
to study under me?

That very moment I'd have turned –
are you listening, student? –

into a salamander of
gold, a silver Undine.
We could have huddled on the rug
before a blazing fire –

the night, the fire, and the moon's face…
Are you listening, student? –

No way of stopping me – my horse
loves galloping crazily! –
package on package, I'd have thrown
the past upon the fire:

old roses, books gone out of date –
Are you listening, student? –

And, when finally the heap
of ashes would subside –
my God, then what a miracle
I'd have made out of you!

An old man reborn as a youth! –
Are you listening, student? –

When, yet again, you threw yourself
into science's trap,
I could have been seen standing there,
rubbing delighted hands

feeling you had become – immense!
Are you listening, student?

*June 1st 1913*

Off with you! I'll not part my lips,
since words are useless here.
The tribunal where they'd pronounce
me right does not exist.

Enchanting coward, darling youth,
I'll be no casualty
in this battle – power isn't what
I fight for in this world.

My highborn verses do not seek
any dispute with you.
You may fail to see my eyes,
because of others, may

resist being blinded by my fire,
indifferent to my strength
and to the demon inside me,
your chance forever lost!

But don't forget – an arrow-sharp
judgement day will arrive,
and then you'll see two wings of flame
shining above my head.

*July 11th 1913*

## To Asya

1

We're on the ball, quick off the mark,
two cutting edges.
Each look, word, gesture makes it clear
we must be sisters.

Our kindness unpredictable,
delicate too.
We're like two whetted sword blades forged
in old Damascus.

No hint of threshing-floors, or loads
of grain, or oxen!
We're like a pair of arrows aimed
directly skywards!

We, in a world of bartering,
alone are sinless.
We're like two verses from a play
by William Shakespeare.

*July 11th 1913*

2

We are the raiment poplars wear
when springtime comes,
in us you see the final chance
offered to kings.

The bottom of an ancient goblet,
look, we are there:
in it you can see your dawn
and our dawns too.

Pressing your lips against it, drink
the contents down.
Once it's been emptied, you'll catch sight
of our two names.

Our bright gaze challenges and dares,
when hostile too.
Who among you failed to meet it
here upon earth?

We stand guard over cradles, over
mausoleums, the last thing
kings' eyes behold.

*July 11th 1913*

# To Sergey Efron-Durnovo

## 1

Voices exist that force you to
fall silent, not repeat their words,
guessing that wonders are in store.
Certain immense eyes exist
the sea's colour.

See, he arose in front of you:
gaze at the forehead, the eyebrows,
then compare him with yourself!
The lassitude, colour sky-blue,
of ancient blood.

The blue of highborn lineage
triumphing in every vein.
Lacework patterns of white foam
repeat the gestures of a prince
or else a lion.

A dragoon taken from your ranks,
Decembrists, fighters at Versailles!
Too young for us to guess what fits
these fingers best – an artist's brush,
a sword, or strings.

*Koktebel', July 19th 1913*

## 2

Limbs like seaweed tentacles,
or branches of Malmaison willows…
You lay there in the splashing foam,
observing absent-mindedly

the melons' flesh of pallid gold
with eyes coloured blue-green, grey-blue,
aquamarine and chrysoprase,
but never opened more than half.

Arrows of salt flew through the air,
the waves were like lions enraged.
You lay there, excessively white,
because the blue could not be borne…

With at your back a wilderness,
somewhere in it, Dzhankoy village,
the melon gold and calm beneath
the tapering fingers of your hand.

You lie there, not deigning to look,
utterly precious, all at peace,
yet should you glance – armies burst into
flame, mountains enter the sea,

unheard of moons begin to burn,
lions rejoice in telling lies –
all you have to do is move
your young, endlessly lovely head.

*August 1st 1913*

# To Byron

I think about the morning of your fame,
the morning of your days,
you wakening like a demon out of sleep,
for the people, a god.

I think of how your eyebrows came together
above those torch-like eyes,
the ancient blood that circulated through
your veins, a lava flow.

I think of you running through wavy hair
those long fingers of yours,
of all the eyes that thirsted after you
in lanes and restaurants,

of hearts in which, given you were so young,
you had no time to read,
of days in which moons would arise and set
as a tribute to you.

I think about a room darkness half fills,
velvet inclined towards lace,
of all the poems you would have declaimed
to me, and I to you.

A fistful of dust, too, all that remains
from your lips and your eyes…
Of all the eyes that now lie in the tomb,
about those eyes and us.

*Yalta, September 24th 1913*

## Meeting with Pushkin

As I climb up the white road,
dusty, resonant and steep,
my nimble legs never get tired
of dangling high above the drop.

To the left – Ayu-Daga's sheer
ridge, a blue abyss all round.
These lyrical surroundings' curly-
haired enchanter comes to mind.

He's on the road, or in a cave,
a swarthy hand raised to his brow.
A cart which bullocks pull gives out
a glass-like tinkle at the turn…

A childhood smell of burning wood
comes from some family or other's fires…
Enchantments of an old Crimea
from the darling times of Pushkin.

Pushkin! You'd understand at once
who stood before you on the path.
Smiling, you would not suggest
I climbed the mountain on your arm.

Not leaning on your swarthy hand,
I would explain as we walked on,
how deep my scorn of learning is,
how I reject authority,

how much I love banners and names,
hair and voices, vintage wines,
thrones no longer occupied –
and every dog crossing my path!

Questions that in answer get
nothing more than a faint smile,
young kings, a burning cigarette,
alleys deep in velvet groves,

play-actors, jingling tambourines,
gold and silver, and the name
I bear, Marina, quite unique,
how I love Byron, a *bolero*,

talismans, candles and cards,
phials, the smell of nomad camps
and fur, love lying words that pierce
the soul, from lips that cast a spell.

Words like "never" and "forever",
the ruts wheels leave upon a road,
dark blue rivers, swarthy hands –
Mariula you wrote about!

Drumbeats, a ruler's uniform,
a palace, carriage windows, groves
that gleam between the jaws of a
fireplace, or a rocket's red stars…

My own undying heart, fealty
to the one and only king!
My heart, and my reflection in
a mirror – I love all of these!

Of course… I would no longer talk,
do nothing more than gazing down
while you, silent, appealing, sad,
embraced a slender cypress tree.

We'd both be silent – am I right?
Watching how, somewhere at our feet,
a first fire sparkled into life
in some Caucasian peasant's house.

And since, however painful sorrow
gets, fun's just a step away,
we'd burst out laughing, and then run
right down the mountain, hand in hand.

*October 1st 1913*

That pit gaping far off already swallowed
so many up!
The day will come when I, too, disappear
off the earth's face.

Whatever sang, put up a fight, shone clear,
tore itself free
will grow stiff – my green eyes, my tender voice,
my golden hair.

Life will continue, with its daily bread,
oblivious days,
everything will go on as if there hadn't
once been a me!

Like children, changeable in every mood,
quick to forget
anger, loving the hour when in the fire
wood turns to ash,

cellos, riding deep into the forest,
and village bells…
I who was so alive, totally here
on loving earth!

I turn to all of you – indifferent to
measure, who cares
if known to me or not? – demanding trust,
begging for love,

by day, by night, writing, in speech, so I
can have my say,
because I was so often hugely sad
aged twenty years,

because there was no way I could avoid
forgiving wrongs,
because my tenderness was unrestrained,
my gaze too proud,

because it all passed by so rapidly,
of truth, of games…
Listen to what I'm saying! Love me too
because I'll die.

*December 8th 1913*

Sensitive, quick to rage, and clamorous –
that's how I long
to be – captivating, intelligent and
irresistible!

More tender than the living or the dead,
stranger to guilt!
It makes me so indignant – in the grave
we're all the same!

Becoming something nobody could love –
turning to ice! –
kept in the dark regarding what happened
and what comes next.

Forgetting how my heart was broken and
then healed again,
forgetting my own voice, the words it said,
my shimmering hair,

how on this arm of mine, as slender as
it's long, as on
a spindly stalk, I used to wear an old
turquoise bracelet…

How, while busy sketching a small cloud
somewhere far off,
a rivulet coloured mother of pearl
decoyed my hand,

how my legs tensed to take a leap across
a wattle fence
and how my shadow, keeping pace with me,
ran down the road.

Forgetting flames within an azure sky,
those quiet days...
all the crazy things I did, the storms and
all my poems!

The wonder overtaking me will put
laughter to flight,
I, who was always rosy-cheeked, will be
palest of all.

My eyelids will stay firmly closed, even when –
oh, pity me! –
they should open to view the setting sun,
to meet a gaze

or else to look upon the open fields,
to see a flower!
Forgive me, my dear native land, forgive
until time ends.

One waning moon, another then, will fade
and snows will thaw
when this enchanting, youthful life of mine
has darted past.

*Feodosiya, Christmas Eve 1913*

# To the Generals of 1812

*for Sergey*

You, whose flapping military
cloaks reminded one of sails,
spurs jangling no less cheerfully
than your voices,

whose gaze, a diamond's cutting edge,
etched an outline on the heart,
dandies no-one could resist
in years gone by,

conquering with gritted teeth
women as you did fortresses,
ruling over battlefields
then at a ball,

defended by God's palm, and by
a mother's heart, one day the merest
striplings, on the following
day, officers.

For you all mountain peaks were small,
the hardest of old bread was soft,
young generals, commanders of
your destinies!

―――――――――

How can I forget the splendid
instant when, fourth Tuchkov, peering
at a faded print, I glimpsed
your tender face,

glimpsed your build, so delicate,
the glitter of your decorations…
I kissed that print, and after could
not get to sleep.

I can't help thinking how your hand,
with all its rings, would have caressed
a young girl's tresses – as it did
your horses' manes.

In one incredible gallop
living through your brief existence
after which snow piled up on your
curls and whiskers.

Three of you vanquished fifteen score!
Only the dead won't fight again.
Children and heroes, capable
of everything.

What could be more affecting than
your youthful frenzy, waging war?
Golden-haired Fortune led you by
the hand, a mother.

Victorious, in love with love
and with your sabres, keenly-honed,
you passed cheerfully over into
non-existence.

*Feodosiya, December 26th 1913*

An unrepeatable spring day
expires on Feodosiya
and the enchanting twilight hour
lengthens shadows all around.

Choking on my misery,
I walk on, mind entirely blank,
letting two frail, abandoned arms
dangle down along my sides.

I meet the kisses of the wind
by the Genoese fortress walls;
around my knees, my dress's silken
folds billow continually.

The rim of my ring is so plain,
the few wild violets I hold
in a bunch close to my face
are poignantly small and forlorn.

I make my way along the fortress
ramparts; the spring evening's filled
with misery, lengthening shadows, and
hopelessness searching for words.

*Feodosiya, February 14th 1914*

Through a linden tree plantation –
extensive, ancient, innocent –
I wander with my mandolin
(my dress as long as long can be)

breathing warm aromas wafted
from corn and ripening raspberries,
the neck of the old instrument
almost slipping from my grasp,

a parting between my curls…
– Rustling from silk drawn tight,
a corsage that is deeply cut,
my skirt gathered in sumptuous folds. –

My gait is languid and exhausted,
my posture like a pliant staff,
I move towards a pedestal
before which somebody lies prostrate.

How pale the quiver and the bow
there where they've tumbled to the grass!
My narrow heel keeps stumbling upon
arrows nobody can see.

There, on a gentle eminence,
behind a stone perimeter,
restored to winter evermore
and redolent of ancient Greece,

time-encrusted, as with ice,
surviving through some miracle,
a mansion with twelve pillars stands,
with terraces, a pond beneath.

Above each pillar in the row
a double whorl raises itself,
each of a dozen windows burns
with a brilliance diamond-bright.

Wasted effort knocking there:
no shadow is seen in the halls
or in the gallery, the sunlit
pond would sooner answer back.

———————————

"Tell me, where are you, tender Count?
Have you forgotten Chloe, Daphnis?"
A wave crosses the pond, welcomes
what's living, following what once was.

Welcomes, too, in a chill embrace,
with a lapping of the waters,
the living roses on my shoulders
and the blossoms on my dress,

lips more crimson still than roses,
my eyes – flowers amidst the leaves…
– As it sinks, my golden hair
in the water's still more golden.

———————————

Day without passion or thought,
a spring day in the antique style,
a young woman's dress rustling
as it brushes ruined steps…

*January 2nd 1914*

# S. E.

Wearing his ring's like throwing down a gauntlet.
If I'm his wife, it's for eternity,
not just on paper. His face, far too narrow,
could be a sword.

His mouth, laconic, turns down at the corners,
his chiselled eyebrows speak of suffering.
His features show the tragic confluence
of two old bloods.

He's thin, but with the thinness of fresh branches.
His eyes – so exquisite, so otiose! –
are two chasms, beneath the outstretched wings
of his forehead.

I'm loyal to that face's chivalry,
to all those fearless lives, and fearless deaths.
In fateful epochs, his kind go two ways –
they compose stanzas, or else mount the scaffold.

*Koktebel', June 3rd 1914*

# To Alya

## 1

Slender, innocent, enchanting,
a mystery to everyone,
a captivating Amazon,
a noblewoman who can't brook

delay – that's who you're going to be,
wearing your hair as if it were
a helmet, queen at every ball,
and of all poems young men write.

Princess, your sarcastic wit
the undoing of more than one,
what I can only dream about
is fated to lie at your feet.

Everyone will pay you homage,
falling silent in your presence.
There's no arguing, you'll write poems
just like I do, only better…

Who can tell, though, if one day you'll
grip your temples with the very
desperation your young mother
feels as she grips hers today?

*June 5th 1914*

## 2

Yes, I'm already jealous of you,
and with what a jealousy!
Already I disturb you with
my melancholy.

My ill-starred nature is already
catastrophically clear
in you. You'll soon be two years old,
and you're so sad.

All the dolls in the world, all the
horses turned down unthinkingly,
you only want a page from my
notebook, a pencil.

It seems you declared war on nannies,
you want to do it all yourself,
suddenly inconsolable:
"the sea went home".

No way to convey what you're like –
however much pride in my words –
when you ask your mother to kiss you
on the "muzzle".

You know how I am filled with glee
each time it proves impossible
to talk you into giving some-
body a kiss.

A dragon, snake carrying off
a princess, or all bridegrooms' bridegroom –
that's me! Light of my eyes, and my
nights' jealousy!

*June 6th 1914*

# To P. E.

1

Without a sound, the August day
dissolved in golden evening dust.
Clanking, trams went on their way,
people strolled past.

Absorbed in thought, I wandered down
a quiet lane. I could have been
going nowhere – I remember bells
chiming, subdued.

Trying to picture how you'd look,
unable to make up my mind
which would be better – to buy you
a rose, or not –

endlessly preparing a phrase
I then – alas! – forgot to use,
without warning I found myself
right at your house.

An utterly dull tenement…
I counted windows, found the door.
Unthinkingly, my hands reached for
my neck, the cross.

I counted step after grey step,
leading me on towards a fire.
There was no time for second thoughts.
I rang the bell.

I still recall its thundering peal,
my hands that were as cold as ice.

I said your name: "Yes, he's at home.
He'll be right there."

======

With youth, may the years sweep away
everything that I can't forget,
such as, the coloured patterns of
that wallpaper,

the little beads on the lampshade,
mysterious voices murmuring,
the prints with views of Port Arthur,
the chiming clock.

A minute, infinitely long,
felt like an hour. Steps from afar,
doors creaking as they opened – you
entered the room.

=======

The charm was instantaneous.
You bowed as simply as a king.
Your eyes, a pair of dark stars, shone
fearfully bright,

immense. You, so appealing, failed
to understand, screwing them up,
the tempest they provoked in me still
for a moment.

I put up a heroic fight
– the two of us had eaten soup! –
I remember a muffled voice
and your mouth's shape.

Your hair, softer than fur, the lines
laughter – so typical for you! –
had traced enchantingly around
your languid eyes.

I still remember, though you won't,
where you were sitting, where I sat,
how I had to master myself
whole minutes long,

sitting, puffing circles of smoke,
remaining utterly at peace –
I found it quite unbearable
to sit like that.

You must remember how we talked
of weather, and of spelling rules.
Never has there been such a strange
lunch encounter.

Half turned away, in the shadows
I surprised myself by laughing:
'Eyes fit for a pedigree
dog – Count, forgive!'

========

Lost in thought, I wandered down
the darkening lane. I could have been
going nowhere. But I think the bells
had stopped chiming.

*June 17th 1914*

## 2

Breakers curling around the cliffs –
protracted, sumptuous din of froth –
it was a child showed me the way
to your cottage.

I couldn't help slowing my pace
as if it would be wrong to rush –
in my ears, the background noise of
grinding pebbles.

A peasant wagon with no canvas
flap creaked past. Beyond the ivy's
green, on the verandah, two
white columns gleamed.

Things can never get so peaceful
except on July afternoons.
I remember you, sprawled in
a wicker chair.

The world's so vulgar! Nobody
knew how to give the just weight to
your captivating pose, a rose
between your lips.

You didn't raise your head – that showed
how absolutely bored you were –
your gesture, when we shook hands, took
my breath away.

Screwing up your exquisite eyes
for some cause nobody can tell,
you knew who was the thunder in
my blue sky now.

Was it the sunlight, or the heat?
The entire garden glowed like amber.
A Tartar came by, selling veils,
went on his way…

Your arrogant, seductive lips
were closed tight – everything was clear.
The sun projected patterned shadows
through thick ivy.

I forget nothing: your straw hat
perched on the edge of the *chaise-longue*,
strident clanging from a gong,
the fragrance of

overloaded, wilting roses,
how the hangings fell, like sails,
our conversation as we smoked,
the faint noise when

you, a prophet, infallible,
tipped your ash out on the roses,
your outfit, too, impeccable
and oh, so bright.

*June 28th 1914*


3

## To His Daughter

Your wings delivered you the same
moment the swallows arrived,
a little body prompting joy,
and two new eyes.

The fact that you were born in March –
– praise be to God! – indicates here
on earth you had a destiny
just like a bird's.

Swallows darted across the sky,
inside the house, chaos prevailed:
babbling children, and beyond the
panes, birds chirping.

Days in November are so short,
November nights so long drawn out.
Those so endearing pale grey wings
are overseas!

A small heart finds it hard to cope
with the harsh cold of northern lands.
That's why the swallows took this nestling
on their journey.

The funeral wreath lies, unmoving
as your delicate eyelashes.
Sleep, child. God's baby fledgling, sleep.
Rock, rock a-bye.

*July 12th 1914*


4

War, war! Incense at the icon cases,
jangling of spurs.
But what to me are emperors' calculations,
nations in strife?

I'm a small dancer on a rope which they
tell me is frayed.

Shadow of someone's shadow. Sleepwalker
of two dark moons.

*Moscow 16th July 1914*


5

You loved him when he was alive
and swore you never would betray him:
fetch lily garlands, spread them out
on the fresh snow.

Linger briefly here, where he
found a poor lodging, in the hope
he won't shiver too much, after
the first snow falls.

With breath from souls and bodies, bring
some warmth back to his frozen blood!
If you managed to damp the flames
of ardour for

the lover, try to love the brother,
the child whose brow carries a wreath –
there's no one for him to hold close
inside his grave.

Each one of you loved him so much
that you'd have braved Hell's gates for him –
don't blame him for being buried now –
it's not his fault!

Steps above him, rustling dresses
set him trembling head to toe –
how wide he'd spread his arms to hug
you, if he could!

Women! He was all for each
of you – ardour, insanity!
Recall how searingly intense
his loving was!

Recall how eagerly you stalked
each single glance of those two eyes,
recall the pledges you once made
in darkest night.

That ought to stop you breaking faith
next to this wretched cross of his;
without saying a word, recall
how those lips kissed.

Before you beat a swift retreat
in a sleigh with small gipsy bells,
linger, kneel, let your faces brush
the night-time snow,

so the light flakes powder your cheeks
and turn to teardrops in your eyes…
I too, writing these verses down,
have joined your ranks.

I cannot breach an oath not sworn –
Life! You have chestnut-coloured eyes! –
Say a prayer, women, for the soul
of Love itself.

*August 30th 1914*

## 6

Fallen leaves gather in heaps on your grave,
there's a chill in the air.
Listen, from where you lie darling and dead
– You've not stopped being mine!

You laugh. You're so smart in that travelling cloak!
The moon's riding high.
Indisputably, incontrovertibly mine
as this very hand is.

Once again I set off for the hospital doors
with a bundle at dawn.
You have merely departed for sunnier climes,
for the unbounded seas.

But I kissed you, cast spells for your sake! I guffaw
at the gloom beyond death!
Death's a sham! I'll be waiting when your train comes in
so we two can walk home.

What matter the leaves, or the words on the bands
fading out, washed away?
If you are dead for the whole of the world,
I must be too.

I see you, I feel, smell you everywhere now,
in spite of the ribbons and wreaths!
I haven't forgotten you. I never will,
right up till the end of the world!

I know that such promises carry no weight,
know their pointlessness, too.
They're a letter to endlessness, limitlessness,
in the post to a void.

*October 4th 1914*

7

Treasured friend, your journey took you farther
than overseas. I've brought you roses. Stretch
your hands out for them. Friend, you carried with you
an earthly hoard dearer than all the rest.

I've been taken advantage of, been robbed,
without a letter or a ring as keepsake,
I who recall even the smallest dimple
on a face eternally surprised,

the fixed stare, filled with leavetaking, as you
invited me to take a closer seat,
the smile from somewhere immense and far off,
the sacred rapture of one in death's arms.

Treasured friend, your cruise will be unending
– freshly dug mound amidst the other humps!
Pray for my sake, on reaching heaven's harbour,
that no-one else may set sail as you did.

*June 5th 1915*

# To Germany

Offered as prey to the whole world,
no way to count your enemies.
How could I leave *you* in the lurch?
How could I betray *you* now?

What to me is common wisdom?
"Eye for an eye, tooth for a tooth"?
Germany, my delirium!
Germany, Germany my love!

How could I repudiate
my persecuted *Vaterland*
as long as, with a narrow face,
Kant roams the streets of Königsberg,

as long as, dandling a new
*Faust*, *Geheimrath* Goethe, in
another small, forgotten town,
walks down a path, grasping his stick?

How could I abandon you,
Germany, star of my heavens,
seeing I was never taught
to love by halves, if ecstasy

invades me on hearing your songs,
oblivious to lieutenants' spurs,
if I revere the statue of
St George on Freiburg's *Schwabentor*,

choked by no hostility
towards your Kaiser's buoyant whiskers,
if I'll bow down in love to you,
Germany, till the day I die.

Nowhere's wiser, more magical,
fragrant than where the Lorelei
combs out her golden hair above
the Rhine flowing on endlessly.

*Moscow, December 1st 1914*

# To My Grandmother

Your face's lengthened, resolute
oval, the flares of your black skirt…
Grandmother! You're so young! Who can
have kissed those haughty lips of yours?

Those hands, performing Chopin waltzes
for royalty in palace rooms…
Spiral ringlets on either side,
framing a face that's frozen, stiff.

Your dark, unwavering, demanding
eyes prepare for an attack.
That's not the way young women gaze.
Who are you, youthful grandmother?

You took so much that might have been,
that never could have been, with you
into the yawning, hungry earth,
a Polish woman, dead at twenty!

The day was guiltless, the wind fresh.
The stars that got put out were dark.
This savage rebel in my heart,
grandmother – it has to be you!

*September 4th 1914*

# With a Woman

## 1

Are you happy? You don't need to tell me. You can't be.
Look, I never asked.
Lips in such numbers have pressed against yours
it's no wonder you're sad.

In you I find each tragic heroine from Shakespeare,
combined into one.
Young in years and a lady, your destiny's tragic –
with no saviour in sight!

Now you know it by heart, you've grown tired of repeating
love's recitative.
The ring of cast iron on your bloodless finger
says all that it takes.

Like a cloud filled with thunder, sin hovers above you.
I've fallen in love
with you. Why? For your burning sarcasm, because
you stand out from the rest.

The lives that we lead, and we two, are so different.
All paths lead through darkness.
You're a temptress of genius, yet not the less helpless
when struggling with fate.

I love you because I must ask your forgiveness,
demon with the steep brows,
because – whatever you do with your life –
you can never be saved.

Because of this trembling I can't put a stop to –
it must be a dream –

because, with a rapture I can't quite believe in,
you aren't a he!

*October 16th 1914*


2

Huddled beneath the woollen plaid
I relive dreams of yesterday.
What happened? Who came out on top?
Who was the loser?

I think it all over again,
the same torment returns.
In something I can't find the words
for, did love play a part?

Who was the hunter? Who the prey?
It's devilishly back to front!
How much did the Siberian cat,
that kept on purring, understand?

During that self-willed hand to hand
which of us merely held a ball?
Whose was the heart – yours, was it mine –
that soared into the sky?

Again the question – What was that?
Desire fulfilled? Pretext for pain?
I still can't work it out. Was I
the winner, or the loser?

*23 October 1914*

**3**

The thaw began today, I spent
a long time at the window.
My eyes weren't swimming, I could breathe
more freely, peace returned.

Who's to say why? I had grown tired,
perhaps, of turbulence
and felt no need to reach a hand
for that rebellious pencil.

I spent a while, equally far
from good and ill, in gloom,
drumming my fingers on a pane
that gave the faintest tinkle.

Nothing mattered much to me,
not the first passer-by,
not puddles of mother of pearl
the skyline spilled into,

not the songbird flying by,
the dog just running past.
Even the beggar woman's song
brought no tears to my eyes.

I'm mistress now in the sweet art
of learning to forget.
Some great feeling I cannot name
thawed inside me today.

*23 October 1914*

4

You couldn't bother getting dressed
or up out of your armchair.
Yet every day you had ahead
my fun would have made full of fun.

You really drew the line at going
out so late into the cold.
Yet every hour you had ahead
my fun would have made full of youth.

You did that all innocently,
what cannot be put right –
as for me, I was the days
of your youth passing by.

*October 24th 1914*


5

Today, close upon eight, headlong
down the Main Lubyanka, like
a bullet or a lump of snow,
a sleigh shot past, going who knows where.

Laughter lingered in the air…
I couldn't take my eyes off you:
a shock of chestnut hair like fur,
someone tall sat at your side!

I'd already been replaced!
The sleigh ploughed onwards, carrying
the woman you love and desire –
one who's more desired than me!

'Oh, je n'en puis plus, j'étouffe!'
you cried in ringing tones, and tucked
her up in the fur travelling rug
with an energetic movement.

A joyous world, a gallant night,
the things bought toppled from your muffs…
Through the blizzard you two sped on,
your gazes meeting, and your furs.

A savage uprising occurred,
the falling snow piled white in drifts.
My eyes followed you for about
two seconds – definitely no more.

Without a trace of anger, I
smoothed the long fur on my coat.
Oh Snow Queen out of Andersen,
your little Kay had turned to ice!

*October 26th 1914*


6


She cries over the coffee grounds
all night, and gazes towards the East.
Loose and innocent, her lips
resemble some peculiar flower.

Soon reddening twilight will yield
its place to a young, slender moon.
You cannot guess how many combs
and rings you're going to get from me!

The moon among the branches there
couldn't keep anybody safe!

I'll give you such a lot of bracelets,
chains, ear-rings on top of that!

From beneath its heavy mane
your horse's pupils sparkle brightly!
Your jealous fellow-travellers?
Swift-footed and pure-blooded steeds!

*December 6th 1914*


7

The snowflakes shone so merrily
on your grey, on my sable fur
as we looked for the gaudiest
ribbons in the Christmas market.

I gobbled no fewer than six
rose-coloured waffles – sugarless!
And petted every chestnut horse
to show how much I adored you.

In russet long coats broad as sails,
swearing, they sold us worthless trinkets,
those foolish women wondering at
the fine, strange ladies down from Moscow.

When people started going home,
we found ourselves inside the church.
You couldn't take your eyes away
from an old icon of God's mother:

that haggard face with gloomy eyes,
benevolent, set in a frame
of podgy cherubs from the days
of the Empress Elizabeth.

Letting my hand slip out of yours,
you gasped "I want her!" Then you placed
a yellow candle, with the utmost
care, inside its candle-holder...

Unpriestlike, with an opal ring,
hand of my whole catastrophe!
I gave you my word I'd come back
and steal the icon that same night.

Into the convent's guest quarters –
nightfall, din of pealing bells –
blissful as if on our name-days
we clattered, like a troop of soldiers.

I swore to grow more beautiful
as I got older, poured out salt,
while you were furious that the King
of Hearts should come three times for me.

Clasping my head in both your hands,
you gave each curl its own caress
then, with the little flower on your
enamel brooch, you chilled my lips.

I led your slender fingers down
the contours of my sleepy face;
you teased me I was like a boy,
told me that was how you loved me...

*December 1914*


**8**


Like a recent shoot, the neck
lifts without restraint.

Who can say her name, how old
she is, her land, epoch?

The sombre lips assume a curve
capricious and weak-willed
and yet the brow, like Beethoven's,
emerges blinding, bright.

Her face's melting oval is
so pure it moves to tears,
her hand looks fit to grasp a whip,
an opal silver-framed.

That hand which ought to bend a bow
vanishes into silks,
a hand that is beyond compare,
peerlessly beautiful.

*January 10th 1915*


## 9

You go down your appointed path –
I won't attempt to touch your hand,
but my pain is too infinite
for me to treat you like a stranger.

My heart leapt towards you at once,
without even knowing your name,
I guessed it all, forgave it all –
Love me, I beg you, just love me!

Your pursed lips and your arrogance
pushed to the limits, make it clear,
your ponderous, projecting brows –
your heart's bent on taking by storm!

Your dress of silk, a black cuirass,
the gypsy hoarseness in your voice –
I love it all so much it hurts –
even that you're not beautiful!

No winter comes for looks like yours!
No blossom, you're a stalk of steel.
Knife-sharp ill-will personified,
what island were you kidnapped from?

Whether a fan shows your caprice,
or else a cane, each vein, each bone,
each finger's grim outline exudes
feminine grace, a boy's defiance!

Parrying laughter with a verse
I proclaim to the world and you,
stranger with Beethoven's brow,
all that you hold in store for me!

*January 14th 1915*


## 10

How could I forget the scent
of "White Rose" mingling with tea,
the Sèvres porcelain figurines
perched above a blazing hearth…?

I was in a party dress
of ribbed silk with a hint of gold,
you wore a jacket, knitted, black,
with a collar ending in wings.

I recall how your face was
when you arrived – no hint of make-up,
how you rose, biting your finger,
head ever so slightly bent.

Your forehead, proof you longed for power,
that weighty helmet, your red hair,
no woman, yet not quite a boy –
in either case, stronger than me!

Without a pretext I got up,
people were standing all around us.
Provocatively, someone said:
"You two ought to be introduced".

Taking your time about it, you
placed your hand in mine, and for
a moment a sliver of ice
dallied, coquettish, on my palm.

Someone looked disapprovingly,
I felt a skirmish imminent
where I lay, half-slouched, in my chair,
twisting my ring round and around.

You produced a cigarette.
I struck a match, gave you a light,
not knowing quite how I'd react
were you to look me in the face.

I remember how our glasses
clinked over a pale blue vase:
"I beg you, please – be my Orestes!"
And I offered you a flower.

Summer lightning in grey eyes.
Not hurrying about it, you

extracted from your black suède bag
a handkerchief – and let it fall.

*January 28th 1915*


## 11


Beneath the sun all eyes breathe fire,
one day's not like another.
Let me tell you, in case I'm ever
unfaithful to you:

It makes no difference whose the lips
I kiss in love's hour are,
it makes no difference who I swear
grim oaths to at black midnight,

saying I'll blossom like a flower,
subservient to a mother's will,
not turn my eyes to right or left
to look at anyone…

See this cross of cypress wood?
Take that as your sign
it's all a dream – whistle beneath
my window without fail.

*February 22nd 1915*


## 12


Close to Moscow the hills are wreathed in blue,
dust and tar in the air, a touch of warmth.
Sleeping, laughing all day, I must be
recovering from the illness that was winter.

I return home as quietly as I can –
who cares about the poems I've not written?
Rumbling wheels, the scent of roasted almonds
matter far more than any four-line verse.

My mind's so empty that I feel light-headed,
because my heart is exceedingly full!
My days are like wave after small wave passing
beneath a bridge I stand on and look down.

A certain person's gaze is far too tender
in the caressing, barely heated air…
I've just recovered from the winter, yet
the illness that is summer has begun.

*March 13th 1915*


## 13

On the eve of separation,
when love is at an end, I will
repeat that I treasured those hands,
treasured those very eyes of yours

which darted glances here and there
towards whoever caught their fancy,
at the same time demanding I
render account for a chance look,

all of you, so damnably
impassioned – God sees everything! –
retribution was exacted
even for a casual sigh.

It wearies me, but I will add
– you needn't hurry to read this! –

that what was natural for you
grated against my very soul.

There's one thing more I want to say
– no difference – tomorrow we part! –
these lips of mine, till they kissed yours,
could have been a virgin's lips.

Until our eyes met, mine were bright
and unrestrained. I could have been
a five-year-old… Happy all those
whose paths never encountered yours.

*April 28th 1915*


## 14

Names have a scent like flowers that make you dizzy,
glances exist that are like dancing flames…
Mouths exist both dark and labyrinthine,
within them recesses damp and profound.

Women exist whose hair is like a helmet.
Their fragile fans dispense catastrophe.
They're thirty years of age. What was it got you
interested in this Spartan child's soul?

*Ascension Day 1915*


## 15

I want to ask the mirror, filled
with sleep and blurred half-darkness,
where your journey leads you, where
you rest your head each night.

Into view comes a ship's mast,
you walking on the deck…
Mournful fields as evening falls,
you shrouded in train smoke.

Twilit fields as the dew falls,
ravens croaking above…
To the four compass points, I send
my blessing upon you!

*3 May 1915*


## 16

What caught your fancy in the first
was her uncontested beauty,
the glint of henna in her hair,
the mournful lure of a Jew's harp,
gravel grating under hooves,
her neat leap from a horse,
and – set with multicoloured stones –
two inlaid toggles.

In the second – a different one –
the delicate arch of her brow,
the patterned roses in her silken
carpets from Bukhara,
the rings she wore on all her fingers,
the birthmark on her cheek,
the tan white lace could not conceal
and midnight London streets.

There was something in the third
that made you love her too, I'm sure…

Has anything of me survived
in your pilgrim's wandering heart?

*14 July 1915*


## 17


Remember – one strand of my hair
meant more than any other head
to me. Go in peace – you, as well,
and you, and you… All of you, go.

Stop loving me, all of you, stop!
Don't bend over me as day dawns!
That way I can quietly go
outside and stand there in the wind.

*6 May 1915*

Inconsequentiality! My fond
transgression, foe and fellow traveller!
You set the laughter sparkling in my eyes,
set a mazurka pumping through my veins;

you taught me it was pointless keeping rings
whoever life might join me to in marriage –
to make random beginnings at an end,
or else finish things off before they start!

Cross between a blade of grass and steel,
here in the world, where we are all so powerless,
I used a bar of chocolate to heal grief,
and laughed right in the face of passers-by!

*March 3rd 1915*

I'm pleased that you are not in love with me,
pleased that I am not in love with you,
pleased that the heavy globe of earth will never
sail away from underneath our feet.
I'm pleased I can have all the fun I wish,
let my hair down, stop playing with words,
that, if our sleeves should brush against each other,
no blushes come, a suffocating wave.

I'm pleased, too, that you take another woman
calmly into your arms in front of me,
rather than wishing I'd burn in the fires
of hell, for kissing someone who's not you;
because, darling, you don't repeat my darling
name by day or night – when there's no point…
Because they'll never sing an *alleluia*
above us in the silence of a church!

Heartfelt thanks, a sincere shake of the hands
because, not realising what you do,
you love me as I am: because I can
have peace at night, because we rarely meet
at the day's end, don't stroll beneath the moon,
because the sun is not above our heads –
I'm absolutely thrilled you're not in love
with me – alas! – nor I in love with you.

*May 3rd 1915*

Prudence – and insane behaviour,
honour – and infamy,
everything that gives people pause
is present to excess

in me. What gets you into prison
all rolled up into one!
In my hair all conceivable
shades are waging war.

I know the words that lovers murmur –
can reel them off by heart!
Twenty-two years have taught me sorrow's
all you can expect.

I'm innocent and rosy-cheeked
no matter what you say! –
yet nobody's a match for me
when lies need to be told.

It's like a ball tossed in the air,
caught when it starts to fall,
the lying instinct Polish great-
grandmothers bequeathed me.

I do it because in churchyards
the grass grows ceaselessly,
I do it because round the tombs
the eddying snowstorm whirls…

Because of violins – and cars –
because of silks, of fire –
because it hurts me people loved
anyone else but me!

Because it torments me the groom
won't have me for his bride...
For poses struck, for poetry –
in the interests of both! –

my boa's caress on my neck...
How could I fail to lie
seeing my voice becomes so soft
when I don't tell the truth?

*January 3rd 1915*

Voices that played at promises,
glances thunderously black,
fate-bearing lips which, having been
seared themselves, sear other lips –

fighting with you was such fun!
What do you have in store for me
now, though, eyes filled with mockery
and, in your voice, a native chill?

*March 14th 1915*

Ships can't sail on indefinitely,
or nightingales keep singing.
How often have I longed to live,
how often longed to die!

Like a child rising from the board
tired of snakes and ladders,
I'm glad I no longer believe
that other worlds exist.

*May 9th 1915*

What do they see? An overcoat
with a young figure wrapped in it.
Absolutely no-one noticed
how tempestuously it flaps.

Each step of mine is young, precise,
utterly trenchant, like my years.
You perceive in the way I walk
everything that vindicates me.

Heading into eternity,
I can't believe that this spring day
will forget how I run, my crazy
shadow pelting after me.

Such blandishment is in the air
I can't help doubling my speed.
Even though the day is windless,
a wind is blowing round my head!

One porch and then another shoots
by me, the whole world's flying past.
I know my own face all too well.
Its expression is cruel today.

I tear along, incisive as
birds heard crying at midnight.
I could swear my forehead, at this
very moment, parts the clouds!

*Ascension Day 1915*

# To Anna Akhmatova

Bent across the folios, your
slender figure's hardly Russian.
The shawl of Turkish fabric round
your shoulders looks more like a mantle.

One single, broken line of black
could summarise your silhouette.
At the height of fun, you're cold –
depression brings you out in sweat.

Your whole existence a chill fever
posing the question: What is she?
You have the forehead of a young
demon, clouded, ominous.

Good for nothing, you'll wear out
all the young men on this earth,
meanwhile aiming straight at our heart,
arrow-like, an unarmed verse.

It can't have been long after four,
early morning, in sleep's haze –
that was when I fell in love
with you, Anna Akhmatova.

*February 11th 1915*

Someone among my forebears was a fiddler,
a horseman and a thief on top of that.
That's why I'm so unable to sit still,
why you can smell the wind all through my hair!

Swarthy, it must be him who helps me steal
apricots from a cart that bullocks draw;
with curly hair and his aquiline nose,
he has to answer for my passionate fate.

Scratching his head, he watched the ploughman plough,
turning a plucked dogrose between his lips.
Worst of accomplices, in bed he was
artful and expert – but he brought bad luck!

Lover of pipes, of necklace beads, the moon,
of all the young girls in each neighbour's house,
one further attribute comes into mind –
my jaundice-eyed forefather was a coward.

He sold his soul to the devil for a farthing
and kept away from graveyards after dark!
There's one more attribute I can't forget –
the knife he carried tucked inside his boot.

Time and again he popped out from behind
a corner, pounced lithe, cat-like on his prey…
No cause for wonder if he didn't need
to play the fiddle for his livelihood!

He couldn't give a damn for anything –
elusive as old snow in summertime!
That's how one of my forebears played the fiddle,
and that's the kind of poet I became.

*June 23rd 1915*

In a haze incense made bluer,
the panels glittered silver.
A wafted feather, without warning,
found its way to me.

Then all at once our eyes had met.
Your voice – what was the prayer? –
trembled like Bohemian glass
a song is shattering.

Anguish and challenge filled the hour:
like a long cry, you moved,
your lowered face had a lightness
midst waves of blue-grey dark.

It only lasted seconds long:
I cast moorings… My boat set sail…
Rival of mine! I'd known that was
how beautiful you'd be.

*September 22nd 1915*

With incalculable tenderness
because I soon must bid you all farewell,
I take my time carefully to decide
who I am going to leave my wolf's fur to,

to whom the blanket I loved snuggling under,
to whom my greyhound and my slender cane,
who's going to get the silver bracelet, with
amber ornamentation all around…

The notebooks, and the multitude of flowers
it's going to be impossible to keep…
For whom my last rhyme will be written – and
who's to receive the gift of my last night!

*September 22nd 1915*

Ignoring the commandments, I took no
communion – till my funeral rites are sung,
it seems I'll go on sinning passionately
thanks to all my five God-given senses!

Friends! Fellow criminals! Beloved teachers,
who egged me on so irresistibly!
Youths, maidens, trees, constellations, clouds, Earth –
we shall encounter God's judgement together!

*September 26th 1915*

I know the truth! All earlier truths are void!
People were not meant to fight each other
here upon earth. Look! Evening comes, then night.
Poets, lovers, warmongers – *what was the point*?

A wind is rising, dew has fallen, soon
a starry blizzard will freeze in the sky.
We'll all soon fall asleep beneath the earth
who couldn't give each other peace when on it.

*October 3rd 1915*

Two suns are growing chill – have mercy, God!
One in the sky, the other inside me.

How all-encompassing the madness was
– can I forgive myself? – which they provoked!

And both grow chill – their beams no longer scorch!
The one which burned the hotter, chills the first.

*October 6th 1915*

I don't remember who it was
pinned that flower to my coat.
My yearning for passion, sadness
and death cannot be quenched.

I hear it in a cello's tones,
in creaking doors, in clinking
glasses and in jingling spurs,
in cries from evening trains,

when shots ring out during the hunt
or carriage bells pass by –
your repeated summons to me,
all you I did not love!

One consolation still remains:
I'm waiting for the man
who'll understand the thing I need
and shoot me down, point-blank.

*October 22nd 1915*

Gipsy passion for breaking up!
You've barely met – you fall apart!
Resting my head upon my hands
I stare into the night, and think:

no matter who rummages through
our letters, they won't fully grasp
how unfaithful we were, that is,
how deeply faithful to ourselves.

*October 1915*

The moon is full, we wear bear fur,
the little bells dance playfully…
Now is the heart's most carefree hour!
The hour when I dig deep.

Wind in our faces makes me wise,
snow makes my eyes more kindly.
Bright on its knoll, the monastery's
a sacrament of snow.

You, friend, kiss the flakes away
from the sable on my chest.
I gaze on a tree in the field,
the circle of the moon.

Our heads don't come together where
the coachman's back is broad.
I begin dreaming about God,
stop dreaming about you.

*November 27th 1915*

For us the fading
day expired in different places.
Now comes the cruellest
hour for you.

Time of the owls, when
mothers must conceal their nestlings.
You cannot start on
love so soon.

I recall your first
steps in my grim home, the ginger-
bread rooster, and the
willow sprig.

Sick teenager, you
brought with you the smell of forest
mistletoe, of clouds
in the sky!

Your eyes are like a
fawn's. Would you forgive the tears in
them if I went down
on my knees?

We're of the same age.
The soul inside you hasn't died
as yet. But I love
words and rings.

*December 18th 1915*

There they lie, transcribed so hastily,
heavy with suffering and tenderness.
One love after another crucified
each instant, hour, day, year, epoch of mine.

Now I can tell how, far off, thunder peals,
how Amazon spears once more start to glint.
– I can no longer hold a pen! – Two roses
sucked my last drop of blood. My heart is dry.

*Moscow 20th December 1915*

Besides a voice that can rob hearts,
I got my forehead's peerless curve
from Fate. She kissed my lips and said
there was nothing I couldn't have.

The taxes I paid mouths were huge,
I heaped roses on people's graves...
When suddenly Fate's heavy hand
caught at my hair as I flew past!

*St Petersburg, December 31st 1915*

# NOTES

## 'Winged, he approached, and on'

Originally entitled 'The Dying Hour of Marie Bashkirtseff', with reference to the Russian poet and painter (1858–1884) whose posthumously published journals made her a celebrity.

## 'These lines are dedicated to'

As part of the Orthodox rite, a ribbon with a prayer embroidered on it is placed across the deceased person's forehead and buried along with them.

## 'The poems that I wrote so early on'

Tsvetaeva wrote to Yury Ivask in April 1933 that this poem offered 'a template – in advance – for my entire literary (and personal) fate. I knew it *all* – from the moment I was born'.

## To Sergey Efron-Durnovo 1: 'Voices exist that force you to'

Tsvetaeva sees no contradiction in placing participants in the December 1825 St Petersburg revolt against Nicholas I alongside those who defended the French monarch at the time of the Revolution.

## Meeting with Pushkin

Ayu-Daga, the "mountain of the bears", is in south Crimea.

## To the Generals of 1812

The reference is to Aleksandr Alekseyevich Tuchkov (1778–1812), killed at the battle of Borodino, whose father was himself a general. Tsvetaeva's daughter wrote in 1961 that her mother, whose sympathies were already more on Napoleon's side, had bought an exceedingly handsome portrait of this man 'at a flea market in that old Moscow which you know only from poems, whereas I was in time to catch it as a child'. The poet carried it with her into emigration, and back to Russia in 1939.

*'There they lie, transcribed so hastily'*
In 1938-39, Tsvetaeva changed 'lie' to 'fly' and re-dated this
poem to January 1916.

---

These notes are intended to be read in tandem with the
introduction. Information given there is not repeated here. In
preparing both introduction and notes, reference was made to the
still magisterial Simon Karlinsky *Marina Tsvetaeva. The woman,
her world and her poetry* (Cambridge 1985), to the excellent
account of Tsvetaeva's life using mainly her own words, edited
by Tzvetan Todorov and translated by Nadine Dubourvieux
as *Vivre dans le feu. Confessions* (Paris 2005), to E. B. Korkina's
year by year chronicle of the poet's life between 1892 and 1922
(Moscow 2012), to the New York 1980 and Moscow 1994
editions of the poems included here, to the poet's letters and
notebooks, and to Véronique Lossky's French versions in *Poèmes
de Russie (1912–1920)* (Paris 2015).

Lightning Source UK Ltd.
Milton Keynes UK
UKHW011531171122
412366UK00003B/125

9 781848 617315